Social Security Roadmap

The Boomer's Guide to Maximizing Social Security Benefits

Shawn Moran, Jim Sullivan, and Don Deans

Published by Tarkenton Institute, Inc.
3340 Peachtree Road, Suite 2300
Atlanta, Georgia 30326

Cover and Page Design by Absolute Publishing
Printed in the United States

Disclaimer

This publication is designed to provide accurate and authoritative information with regards to the subject matter presented. It is published with the understanding that the publisher and author are not engaged in rendering legal, accounting, or other professional services. If legal, accounting, or other professional advice is required, the service of a competent professional should be sought. Nothing in this book should be construed as a recommendation for the use of products or strategies discussed in any person's retirement plan.

The suitability of any strategy or product is dependent on a person's circumstances, including many factors such as his or her personal and financial goals, net worth, age, risk tolerance and other factors. Every individual should consult with a licensed financial or insurance professional to determine if any financial or insurance product or strategy is suitable for his or her use.

It is customary in financial publications to caution readers that many financial and insurance products are complex and general information about them should not, without adequate study, be applied to specific circumstances. This publication provides such a caution. Although much of the material included is technically accurate, some of the other content is subject to the authors' personal opinions and interpretations, all gleaned from years of practical experience.

The statements made herein regarding Social Security are believed by the publisher to be accurate as of the date of publication. Individuals have a responsibility to verify that any statements made are accurate.

Table of Contents

Introduction

This is a Roadmap to maximizing your Social Security benefits. It is an important topic.

There will be a few fun diversions along the way ("Or, perhaps you don't want to see the second largest ball of twine on the face of the earth which is only four short hours away." – Chevy Chase as Clark Griswold in 1983's *National Lampoon's Vacation*) but don't let that distract you from the seriousness of this topic.

Making the right decision about your Social Security benefits can mean adding tens of thousands of dollars to your retirement income. And that extra money comes when you will need it most – in your later years when you are likely to be frail and suffering from chronic illness. This means extra health care costs – much of which you will have to pay out of your own pocket.

According to a recent study published in the Journal of the American Medical Association (published online at http://jama.jamanetwork.com/journal.aspx, July 10, 2013), our life expectancy has increased. That's the good news. The bad news is that we will spend more of our final years living with a disability.

Social Security has a lot going for it – a steady stream of predictable, inflation-adjusted retirement income. In addition, by delaying receipt of your benefits you will learn that you can increase your monthly Social Security income by 32%. This additional income can provide some protection against rising health costs while also helping you continue to afford your desired standard of living.

All in all, not a bad deal. But to take advantage of Social Security's benefits, Boomers need to learn a little bit about the system. That is the purpose of this book. So, may you...

Live long and prosper. – Dr. Spock (first used in *Star Trek* episode *Amok Time* broadcast September 15, 1967)

In the meantime, read on!

CHAPTER ONE

Boomers Rediscover the Value of Social Security

Remember the famous 1994 poll sponsored by Third Millennium that purported to show more young people believed in UFOs than believed that Social Security would be available when they were ready to file for benefits? Despite the controversy that surrounded the poll results and methodology, the poll has become an urban legend that is still referred to often.

The poll results only seemed to confirm what many Boomers believed at the time (regardless of what they thought about UFOs) – Social Security is of little value and is likely to be gone or greatly reduced by the time Boomers retire. Many financial planners at the time recommended running "what if" retirement income projections for clients without Social Security included or with the amount reduced by at least one-third of expected benefits.

> **Are you a Boomer?**
>
> You are a Boomer if you were born during the period 1946 through 1964. There are 79,000,000 of us. The first Boomers began to reach age 65 in 2011. If you were born before 1946, you are not considered a Boomer. Because the vast majority of those born before 1946 are age 70 or older, many of the planning options we discuss in this book don't apply to you. But if you are married to a Baby Boomer, some of these ideas may still be revelant. Read on...we will keep you in mind as we move forward.

So you are not alone if you have spent the last forty years or so overlooking and underestimating the value of Social Security to your retirement income. Well, things have changed – Boomers have recently rediscovered the value of a monthly Social Security check.

It is easy to see why Social Security is getting a second look:

1. It provides a steady stream of monthly income for life;

2. The benefit is essentially backed by the Federal government (although not guaranteed – there is a difference);

3. After the benefit begins, it is adjusted for inflation annually;

4. It is in relatively sound financial condition (well, at least when compared to Medicare, but that is a separate issue) and it is highly unlikely that any benefit changes will impact Boomers;

5. While Social Security rules are gender neutral, Social Security is especially valuable to women;

6. There are strong protections for divorced spouses.

The six benefits listed above all have great value but you as beneficiary have little control over these - the benefits are already baked into the Social Security cake. There are two other kicker benefits that you do have control over and with proper planning you can often increase your lifetime Social Security payments by tens of thousands if not hundreds of thousands of dollars. These are the kicker benefits:

Kicker Benefit #1: Control over timing

You have the flexibility to choose when to start your benefits, in other words, at an age that best fits your income needs and retirement planning. The longer you wait (you can choose to start your benefit as early as age 62) the bigger your benefit will be. You receive your largest monthly benefit if you can wait until age 70 to begin benefits. In most cases, and for several reasons we will explain, patience is a virtue in deciding when to start your Social Security benefits.

Kicker Benefit #2: Control over your eligibility status

There are several ways you may qualify for beneficiary status – as a worker with a Social Security work record, as a spouse of a worker, as a survivor or as a dependent of a worker. In fact, you may have Social Security rights as both a worker and as a spouse. The amount paid to you in one category may be higher than the amount paid to you in another category. For example, you may be eligible for one benefit based on your work history and at the same time be eligible for a spousal benefit based on being married for over ten years to the same person. You cannot receive both benefits at the same time. But with a little planning you can elect one benefit (such as your spousal benefit) for a period of time at age 66 and strategically switch to your own benefit based on your work record in a later year – say at age 70. What is the benefit to you? Done correctly, you will receive greater lifetime benefits and, if married, provide your spouse greater financial protection if he or she lives a long time following your death.

Our focus in this book will be on the two kicker reasons for taking a closer look at Social Security – in other words, the factors you can control in planning the timing of taking your benefits and deciding your status when you file – worker, spouse, etc. The control you have, so often overlooked, can be worth tens of thousands of dollars in future retirement income whether you are single or married. For those who are married it can also add a measure of longevity protection for the one you love.

But first...

To really get a handle on this, you should have your (and if married, your spouse's) Social Security benefit information in front of you. Go to www.socialsecurity.gov. Once on the home page click on *my Social Security* to sign in or create an account. If you haven't yet set up an account, do so right away; the instructions are easy to follow. Once you sign in to your account you will find your personal information (such as your projected Social Security benefits at various ages) and your wage history since the beginning of time (I really had $1,324 of wages in 1962? Seemed like a lot of money at the time...wasn't 1962 the year the Rolling Stones formed? Talk about looking old...).

With your information in front of you, let's get started.

CHAPTER TWO

The 8 Keys to Maximizing Your Social Security Benefits

The purpose of this book is to help you better understand how Social Security works and use that understanding to maximize your lifetime benefits.

Perhaps the biggest retirement planning mistake you can make is to underestimate the value of your Social Security benefits and make a poorly informed decision regarding *when and how* to take your benefits. The wrong decision can easily cost you tens if not hundreds of thousands of dollars in lifetime benefits. This applies whether you are single, married or divorced.

This may be the single most important book on retirement you will ever read. We were going to name this book, *The Only Social Security Guide You Will Ever Need* but decided that would limit us if we wanted to write a sequel.

Below we've summarized the eight key topics covered in this book that you need to understand in order to maximize your Social Security benefits. For your convenience, we have added where this information is found in the book.

Key #1: You may be *eligible* for benefits in one of the following categories:

- Worker
- Spouse *(or divorced spouse)*
- Survivor
- Dependent

Did you know you may be able to increase your lifetime benefits by electing to take a spousal benefit first and later switching to your worker benefit? Eligibility and benefits paid to you as a *worker* will be based on your work history. Eligibility and benefits paid to you as a spouse depends on the work history of your spouse. (*Find more information in Chapters 3,4,5,6*)

Key #2: You need to know your *full retirement age (FRA)* and how it impacts the *timing* of your benefit election.

For Boomers, FRA is age 66 or later (up to age 67 for Boomers born in 1960 or after). At FRA you receive your full benefit (known as your *Primary Insurance Amount or PIA*) Whether you are single or married, patience may be the key to maximizing your benefits. This means waiting until at least your FRA or even later (see Key #3). While you may be tempted to take your benefit as early as possible, you will be surprised how much that decision may cost you! A delay in taking benefits can also be of significant value to the surviving spouse if the higher-earning spouse dies first. We will tell you why. We take you beyond consideration of the old "break even" analysis of when to begin taking your Social Security benefit. What you learn will put money in your pocket. (*Find more information in Chapters 5,8*)

Key #3: You may elect to take *reduced* benefits as early as age 62; full benefits (your PIA) at your FRA and may take an *enhanced* benefit as late as age 70.

When it comes to maximizing Social Security benefits timing can be *almost* everything. Remember we said that maximizing your Social Security benefits means taking control of not only *when* but *how* you elect benefits? Here is where we tie it all together. (*Find more information in Chapters 5,11*)

Key #4: If you wait until after your FRA to receive your benefit, you can earn an enhanced benefit – for life.

Benefits are *enhanced* by Delayed Retirement Credits (or DRCs) which are applied between your FRA and age 70. DRCs add 8% to your benefit for each full year you delay. After age 70 there is no additional benefit to waiting. Here is one thing most people don't think much about (but should) – the annual 8% increase to your benefit is risk-free. This increase is sweet – where else can you get that type of return – guaranteed? (*Find more information in Chapter 5*)

Key #5: Social Security personnel can help you *apply* but not *strategize*.

Social Security Administration personnel can answer questions about your Social Security benefit but cannot help you figure out a strategy which will provide you (and your spouse, if married) with the largest lifetime benefit. Here is where a knowledgeable advisor and software can come in handy. *Don't just apply, strategize.* (**Find more information in Chapter 5**)

Key #6: Up to 85% of your Social Security benefit may be subject to income tax.

Once you begin receiving your benefit you want to hold on to as much as you can. Learning the rules about how Social Security is taxed can help you keep more of it. (**Find more information in Chapter 10**)

Key #7: Don't lose track of your spousal rights – you earned them.

Spousal rights don't disappear after a divorce. Even if you've been divorced for many years you still may be entitled to benefits based on your ex's work history. We will review the rules so you don't lose out on larger benefits that you may have forgotten about or didn't know you had! (**Find more information in Chapter 7**)

Key #8: It takes careful planning to maximize your Social Security benefits.

If you decide to forgo immediate Social Security benefits in favor of greater long term benefits, you need to plan. This means careful income planning – what source of income can you draw on while you forgo some or all of your Social Security benefit? What is the impact on taking early Social Security benefits if you continue to work? What if you ever worked for wages not covered by Social Security? All of these issues must be carefully considered. The issues impact your taxes, investments, cash flow and even your lifestyle. That is what a good advisor should be able to help you with. This book will get you started! (**Find more information in Chapters 9,12**)

Before we get started here a few odds and ends worth knowing about Social Security *and* Medicare:

☐ While the FRA under Social Security has increased, that is not true of Medicare eligibility – it still begins at age 65.

☐ Your Medicare coverage begins the month in which you turn age 65; Social Security benefits begin the month after you turn age 65.

- But wait! If you were born on the first day of a month both Social Security and Medicare consider that you were born in the month before.

☐ The Social Security Administration handles enrollment for both Social Security and Medicare. You can enroll either online (easiest) or by going to a local Social Security office.

First Boomer to Claim Social Security

According to the Social Security Administration, the first Baby Boomer to apply for benefits was Kathleen Casey-Kirschling. Ms. Casey-Kirschling was born one second after midnight on January 1, 1946. She filed for her benefits on October 15, 2007. By the way, she filed for her benefits online. Notice that because she was born on the first of the month, her benefits actually began in January 2008, not February.

In Chapter 3 we discuss in more detail *how* you can become eligible for Social Security benefits.

CHAPTER THREE

What You Don't Know About Filing for Your Benefits

Social Security recognizes that we fill several "roles" in life. Some of these roles – such as class clown in high school – unfortunately do not entitle us to any Social Security benefits. Other roles we fill – worker, spouse, divorced spouse, dependent, widow/widower may *earn* us Social Security benefits. In this chapter we will focus on those roles we fill that earn Social Security benefits.

An important factor in maximizing your lifetime Social Security benefit is determining how you are going to file. In other words, your status as a beneficiary – worker, spouse, divorced spouse, etc.

What you will discover in this chapter is that you may be entitled to Social Security benefits based on more than one role you filled. For example, a woman may be entitled to a benefit as a worker, as a spouse, or as a divorced spouse. In some cases she may be able to pick whether she wants her Social Security benefit based on her role as a spouse or as a worker. She can't have both but in some cases she can file for benefits based on her role as a spouse and later file for the benefits she earned as a worker.

> **Roles**
>
> Most Boomers remember seeing John Travolta (born in 1954) for the first time in the hit series *Welcome Back, Kotter* which ran from 1975 to 1979. Travolta went on to star in such movies as *Grease* (1978) and *Pulp Fiction* (1994). Few Boomers, however, know that Travolta turned down the lead in both *American Gigolo* (1980) and *An Officer and a Gentleman* (1982). Richard Gere (born in 1949), another Boomer favorite, ended up starring in both movies.

In other words, you have some flexibility as to *how* you file for benefits as well as *when* you file for benefits.

Eligibility for Social Security benefits *as a worker* means you:

1. Worked at a job with wages that had Social Security taxes withheld – in other words, "covered employment." Some wages are not "covered" by Social Security – see Chapter 12. For example, many teachers earned wages that did not have Social Security taxes withheld – their employment was uncovered.

2. Had at least 40 hours of credits – approximately 10 years of work.

You are not required to have a work history to qualify for Social Security benefits. You can, for example, earn a *spousal benefit.* Even if you never worked for pay outside your home you can claim a spousal benefit (as long as you meet certain rules which we discuss in Chapter 6). As we discuss in Chapter 7 you have spousal rights that you are entitled to even if you get a divorce. Likewise, dependents of a worker (children and even elderly parents) can also qualify for benefits upon the death of the worker.

Getting back to the point we made earlier in this chapter - how does this filing flexibility actually work in practice? Let's look at two examples.

Example #1: Ellen is 58 years old, the mother of two adult daughters. She was divorced from their father in 1999 after twenty years of marriage. Since then she has built a career in retail sales. She would like to retire at age 62 and move to be near her daughters and their families in Kentucky. She has never remarried. She filled two roles, both of which entitle her to Social Security benefits – wife and worker. Even though she is now divorced, she has not lost the Social Security spousal rights she earned during twenty years of marriage. As a worker, she has her own work history that is more than sufficient to pay her a Social Security benefit starting as early as age 62. Ellen has three choices:

1. She can file for spousal benefits;

2. She can file for her worker benefits; or

3. She can first file for her spousal benefits and later switch to her worker benefits.

What did Ellen decide? We'll find out in Chapter 7 when we discuss protecting spousal rights.

Example #2: Bob and Amber have been married for over 30 years. Both Bob and Amber have a Social Security work history of their own. At age 66, Bob's Full Retirement Age, he can choose to file for his benefit as a worker or for his spousal benefit. He can also elect to file for his benefit as a worker and then "suspend" actual payment until sometime in the future. He might even wait until age 70 to begin the previously "suspended" payments. Why would Bob suspend being paid the benefits he earned as worker? See Chapter 6 for the rest of the story.

The decision *how* to file for benefits is part of the strategy to maximize your benefits. In the next chapter we will consider *when* to file.

Boomers Shake Up Country Music

1989 saw the emergence of three country music superstars – all Boomers. Dwight Yoakam (born 1956); Garth Brooks (born 1962) and Alan Jackson (born 1958) all had their first big hits that year.

CHAPTER FOUR

Timing is (Almost) Everything

When it comes to your Social Security benefit, you have the greatest flexibility in electing when to begin receiving your benefits. The basic rules are straightforward:

☐ You may file for a *reduced* monthly Social Security benefit **as early as** age 62.

☐ You may file for your *full* monthly benefit at your **Full Retirement Age (FRA)**.

☐ You may file for an *increased* monthly Social Security benefit **as late as** age 70.

For most Boomers the FRA is 66. For younger Boomers (born in 1955 through 1959) their FRA increases gradually until it reaches age 67. For example, for those born in 1955 the FRA is 66 years and 2 months. For those born in 1960 or later the FRA stays at 67.

What is the significance of your FRA? It is this: your Social Security benefit is calculated assuming you begin taking benefits at your FRA. The full monthly benefit you are entitled to at your FRA is your **Primary Insurance Amount** or **PIA**. Your PIA is *decreased* if you take benefits early and *increased* if you take benefits later.

If this all seems simple and straightforward, you probably should go back and read it again. There are a lot of issues you and your advisor need to consider when it comes to the timing of taking your first Social Security payment.

The following example will help you understand your FRA, your PIA and what happens to your PIA if you take benefits before or after your FRA.

Carol is 60 years old. Her FRA is 66. The **Social Security Administration** (or **SSA** – pay attention, another acronym quiz is coming) has estimated her PIA at age 66 as $2,000 per month. Note at this point, it is only an estimate – Carol plans to continue working until age 66 so her monthly PIA will likely change (refer to Chapter 11 on how your Social Security benefit is calculated).

If she were to elect to take benefits at age 62, her monthly benefit would be reduced to $1,500 – a 25% reduction of her PIA. Also note that if she does take benefits early (any time before her FRA) she will be subject to the *earnings test* that will result in her losing some of her Social Security benefit if she continues to work and her earnings are above a certain amount. More on this topic in a later chapter.

If she were to elect to take benefits at age 70 her enhanced benefit would be $2,640, or a 32% increase.

She can elect to begin taking payments at any time between age 62 and 66. At age 62 her benefit would be $1,500 but for each month she delays, her monthly benefit would increase. For example, if she were to wait until age 63 and 3 months to begin taking payments, her monthly benefit would increase by approximately $125 from $1,500 to $1,625.

Once early benefits are begun, the reduction applied to her PIA is permanent. As you will see, this permanent reduction can cause a huge difference in your lifetime benefits – one of the reasons advisors recommend waiting at least until you reach your FRA to begin benefits.

Similarly, if Carol begins her benefits after her FRA but before age 70, her PIA is increased. For example, if she began taking benefits at age 67, her monthly benefit would be $2,160 or an 8% increase for waiting for one year after her FRA. For each year (or portion of a year) after she reaches her FRA that she delays taking a benefit she will receive an 8% increase (or less for a portion of a year) in her monthly benefit.

You can obtain an estimate of your Social Security benefit by going to www.socialsecurity.gov and setting up a my Social Security account.

The Breakeven Point

Deciding when to file for your Social Security benefit is a key part of maximizing your lifetime Social Security benefit. Considerations include:

☐ Do you begin your benefits as early as possible, collecting a smaller check for a longer period of time?

☐ Is it better to wait until age 70 to collect the largest benefit possible even if it is for a shorter period of time?

In this chapter we are just going to consider what a single individual needs to consider when making his or her election to begin benefits. In a later chapter we will demonstrate that married couples have a slightly more complex decision.

For many years, advisors directed their clients to do a "breakeven" analysis when considering the best time to begin Social Security payments. Let's use Carol's example above. She can begin benefits anytime between age 62 and age 70. If she opts for benefits to begin at age 62 she will receive a smaller check than were she to wait until age 66; she would receive an even larger check if she were to wait until age 70. The break even analysis is relatively simple.

At age 62 Carol will receive $1,500 every month for life (we will ignore the annual inflation adjustment). By age 66 she will have received 48 monthly payments of $1,500 (4 years times 12 months per year times $1,500 equals $72,000). Had she waited until age 66 her payments would begin later but would be $2,000 per month or $500 more than the payment she would receive at age 62.

Is Carol better off taking the early benefit? The answer: it depends on how long she lives. If she lives until age 64 there is no question she was better off taking the early benefit. But what if she lives until age eighty or ninety?

The Breakeven Chart below shows the total benefits Carol will receive assuming she elects to start benefits at age 62, 66 (her FRA), or age 70 and she dies at age 80.

Age at which benefit begins	Monthly Benefit	Number of Social Security Monthly Payments to Age 80	Cumulative Benefits Received by Age 80
Age 62	$1,500	18 years x 12 months = 216	$324,000
Age 66 FRA	$2,000	14 years x 12 months = 168	$336,000
Age 70	$2,640	10 years x 12 months = 120	$316,800

This table helps us zero in on the "breakeven point." That is the point where the benefit of receiving payments early is offset by the benefit of receiving larger payments but starting payments later. You can see that give or take a few months, if Carol lives to age 80 she will be better off delaying benefits. By delaying to age 66 she is well ahead in terms of total amounts received by age 80 compared to starting benefits earlier. Starting benefits at age 70 still lags, by a small amount, the cumulative benefits received by starting at age 62 or 66. In just a year or so, however, the cumulative benefits received by delaying taking benefits until age 70 will take the lead over the other two choices – for good.

But the breakeven analysis should *not* be your only consideration. Here some other issues:

1. *Your health* – if you have a chronic disease that may shorten your life expectancy, consider taking your benefits as soon as possible.

2. *Your family's longevity* – do you come from a long line of immortals? If not immortals, at least a mom and dad or grandparents who lived into their 90s or beyond? In that case, consider beginning your payments as late as possible.

3. *Your finances* - do you need the Social Security payment? If you cannot make it month to month without having a Social Security check coming in you may not have the luxury of deciding when to take your benefit.

4. *Invest the early payments* – some advisors may suggest taking the early payments even if you don't need them to make ends meet. These payments are invested and may grow to a nice additional nest egg by the time your reach age 66 or 70. Be careful – the increase in Social Security benefits by delaying is guaranteed by the government. Short of a law change, your increased payments are pretty certain. It is hard to duplicate this type of guaranteed growth in any other investment unless you put the money in a U.S. government note or bond. You may do better in a stock mutual fund but you take on additional risk. So, you may do better, you may not, but to do better you have to take on more risk! Beating the 8% per year DRC increase is very tough to do especially since the DRC is virtually risk-free.

5. *Impact of COLA* – Once your benefits begin, the monthly payment is increased annually by a cost of living adjustment (although recently, inflation was non-existent, so the adjustment was 0%). If you begin benefits early, the COLA is always applied to your smaller payment. With

Carol, for example, if the COLA is 3%, the adjustment to her $1,500 monthly payment is $45 ($1,500 times 3%); the adjustment to her age 66 monthly benefits is $60; the adjustment to her age 70 monthly benefit is $80. Over the years, this creates a larger and larger difference and is another good reason to delay.

6. *Longevity protection* - here is one element of Social Security that is extremely valuable but often overlooked – the longevity protection it provides. This does not fit neatly into the breakeven analysis. The truth is we are all living longer. Social Security, because it pays you a benefit for life, protects you if you happen to live well beyond your life expectancy. If you are age 66 and if your life expectancy is age 80 that means that one-half of those age 66 will not live to age 80; the other half will live beyond age 80. ***Do not overlook this very valuable insurance benefit – if you delay receiving benefits to age 70 for the longevity protection alone, that may be the best possible decision absent health problems or financial need.***

7. *Social Security is going bankrupt so get it while you can* – We believe this is the weakest argument for grabbing benefits early. While Social Security has its financial issues, relatively small changes such as increasing the FRA for those under age 50 or making small changes to the COLA formula can strengthen the system for many years to come. It is possible, although highly unlikely, that Congress would cut back on benefits already being paid. Frankly, we find this excuse used by those who want to take benefits early even if it makes no sense given their situation. If you need something to worry about, worry about Medicare. It is in much worse financial condition than Social Security.

In the last chapter and in this chapter we covered the two most important keys to maximizing your Social Security benefits – *how to file and when to file*. Each requires careful consideration and a basic understanding of the rules. It helps if you can find an advisor who understands Social Security and can walk you through some "what if" scenarios.

Don't go and get all grabby when it comes to your Social Security benefits. A poor decision can cost you tens if not hundreds of thousands of dollars in benefits. A bad decision can also leave you more financially vulnerable as you age. We discussed

Longevity Protection

Going back to our example with Carol, if she lives to age 90 her cumulative benefits if she takes her benefit at 62 will be $504,000. If she delayed to age 70 her cumulative benefits are $633,600 for a difference of almost $130,000. Longevity protection is of real value and should not be overlooked.

situations where taking benefits early makes sense – you have a shortened life expectancy, you can't afford to retire without Social Security and you can no longer work and bring in an income. But for most of us, patience in applying for benefits can pay off big.

For You Gearheads

The first muscle cars arrived just a few years after the first baby boomer. A muscle car is a high-end performance automobile with a powerful engine. Essentially, the idea was to put a large engine in a small car. The 1949 Oldsmobile Rocket 88 is generally considered the first muscle car. That Oldsmobile produced the first muscle car was ironic – it stopped producing cars in 2004 in part because of its stodgy image. Famous muscle cars include the Ford Torino GT; Oldsmobile 442; Pontiac GTO and Dodge Charger RT.

CHAPTER FIVE

The Pause that Refreshes: Why It All Works

Here is where we catch our breath.

In the last two chapters you learned that there is some flexibility when it comes to *how* to file and *when* to file. Now we will focus on *why* understanding these concepts will help you maximize your Social Security benefits.

Before we discuss actual claiming strategies in later chapters, let's do a brief recap to tie it all together for you.

The How - Social Security has several categories of beneficiaries; this is the ***how*** of filing for benefits:

☐ The worker;

☐ The spouse or ex-spouse of a worker;

☐ The dependent of a worker (an underage or disabled child, or an elderly financially dependent parent);

☐ The survivor of a worker (a widow/widower; a child or elderly financially dependent parent at the time of the worker's death).

Note that the various categories listed above all begin with the *worker* – the individual who has earned a Social Security payment based on meeting the Social Security requirements including a sufficient work history. In effect, the worker and his or her work history creates a whole new set of Social Security beneficiaries. They are beneficiaries because of their relationship with the worker – not because they have ever contributed themselves to the Social Security system. It is this part of Social

Security that is not always fully understood or appreciated. That is unfortunate because understanding how the system works can mean greater financial protection.

In addition, to fit into a category and be eligible for benefits, the beneficiary must meet other requirements. For example, for an ex-spouse to receive benefits he or she must have been married to the worker for at least ten years prior to the divorce and must not have remarried before age 60. Special rules apply if the ex-spouse is caring for the child of the deceased.

You may fit into more than one beneficiary category. You may have earned a benefit based on your own work record and be a spouse (or ex-spouse) entitled to spousal benefits. When your spouse dies you become entitled to survivor benefits.

The takeaway for planning purposes: The strategies outlined in the coming chapters may have you file for a benefit in one category and have you switch to another category later. By doing this you may substantially increase your total lifetime benefits.

The When - Social Security gives you flexibility regarding **when** to file for your benefits. In general you may file as early as age 62; you may file when you reach your Full Retirement Age (age 66 to age 67 for Boomers); or you may wait until age 70. If you file early, your benefits will be *decreased* by as much as 25% or 30%. If you file when you reach your FRA you receive your *"full benefits"* or Primary Insurance Amount (PIA); if you file after your FRA but at or before age 70 your benefit will be increased by as much as 32% due to Delayed Retirement Credits (DRCs).

We discussed reasons not to delay your benefit – you are chronically ill and expect to die early; you have no other financial resources to live on until age 67 or 70. But, in general, it is better to delay taking your Social Security benefits for as long as possible. That is because by delaying benefits you receive greater income protection if you live beyond the life expectancy of your age group. We also discussed the "breakeven calculation" and why it has limited value. *The longevity protection offered by Social Security is very valuable and should not be overlooked by you or your advisor.*

The takeaway for planning purposes: Don't go with your first impulse and grab your benefits early. Carefully consider your options, your health and your other financial resources before selecting a date to begin taking benefits.

The Why - Tying It All Together for Planning Purposes: The *how* and the *when* are not independent decisions! For example, under one strategy, it may make sense for you to file for your spousal benefits (*the how*) at FRA (the *when*). This will allow the benefits you earned as a worker to continue to grow thanks to DRCs. Later, when your benefit will no longer receive DRCs for waiting to claim your benefit, you will switch over to your worker benefits (the *how*) at age 70 (*the when*). This strategy can even work for divorced spouses still eligible to file for their spousal benefits on their ex's work record.

The ***why*** for singles is to maximize their lifetime Social Security benefit given an estimate of how long they may live and the availability of other financial resources. For a married couple, the *why* is to maximize their total lifetime Social Security benefits based, in part, on an estimate of the life expectancy of the last to die. In the next chapters we will focus on specific strategies to answer the *why* question.

"The Face of 1966"

Lesley Lawson was one of the world's first supermodels. The London Daily Express named her "The Face of 1966." Born on September 19, 1949, this Boomer is better known professionally as Twiggy. She was known for her *very* thin build. She transitioned from modeling into films such as *The Blues Brothers* in 1980 and television – *America's Next Top Model* from 2005 – 2008. She continues to influence the fashion world working with the international retailer Marks and Spencer. In fact, the "Twiggy effect" refers to older women being more confident about dressing stylishly.

CHAPTER SIX

Strategies for Couples

Bob was in bed lying on his side. He was just about to drift off to sleep when he felt his wife Maggie tap him gently on his back. In more than thirty years of marriage, she always let him know she was "in the mood" with a gentle tap. He slowly turned over to his other side to face her. Ah, he thought, I still have the old magic after all these years.

"Bob," she said, "do you know the most important thing couples our age do together? Coordinate their Social Security benefits."

Bob suddenly woke up, drenched in sweat.

"I've got to stop attending retirement planning seminars," he thought.

Maggie was still soundly asleep. This time Bob tapped her gently on the shoulder.

"In your dreams," she said.

Bob sighed and went back to sleep.

One of the biggest retirement planning mistakes a married couple can make is treating their Social Security elections as unrelated. Husband takes his benefit as early as possible. Wife takes her benefit as early as possible. Just like sleeping in separate beds.

But married couples have a tremendous opportunity to integrate their benefits and at the same time, provide greater income while both are alive and later provide the survivor with not only greater income but also greater longevity protection. Husbands will especially want to understand how to plan and integrate Social Security benefits with their wives, since wives usually outlive their husbands by several years, earn less income over their lifetime than their husbands and also face greater health care expenses as they age due to the need for care as they age and become more frail.

We cannot discuss every strategy that is available to a married couple. That is due, in part, to individual circumstances. A strategy that may work for you and your spouse may not work for another couple. That is where an advisor can find the best strategy that works for you. Your advisor should have access to a software program that can crunch all the numbers. One thing we can promise - you will be surprised at how much difference the right election can make in your retirement income. Don't take your Social Security without some guidance.

Advisor alert! A recent study found that only 20% of financial advisors recommend that the husband delay taking a benefit as long as possible. This demonstrates that many advisors don't know what they are doing when it comes to providing advice on Social Security filing strategies. For more information go to: http://squaredawayblog.bc.edu/squared-away/field-work/social-security-that-harms-wives/

As you will learn below, the key factors in couples' planning are:

☐ Each of your filing status options;

☐ The current age of you and your spouse – some Social Security election options are not available at certain ages;

☐ Whether one of you has already filed for a Social Security benefit;

☐ Your respective ages and expected longevity. The role of the survivor benefit is often ignored when couples plan, to the great detriment of the surviving spouse.

Filing Status Options

In Chapter 3, we discussed how an individual may qualify for Social Security benefits under several different roles he or she plays:

Worker status - based on his or her own Social Security work history.

Spouse status - based on their husband's or wife's work history.

Survivor status - a widow or widower being paid a benefit based on the work history of the deceased.

We also learned in chapters 3, 4 and 5 that you can, in some circumstances, file for benefits under one status (e.g., file first for your *spousal benefit*) and when advantageous, switch to benefits paid under a second status (e.g., later, switch to your *worker benefit*).

Bottom line: Your couple's strategy may involve one (or both) of you making an election under one status and later switching to a second status. But you have to be careful to observe the rules. If you do it incorrectly, you may be limited to which benefit you elect to take.

Some Strategies are Age Dependent

As we discussed previously, the three key Social Security ages are age 62 (the earliest date you can elect a benefit); age 66 (Full Retirement Age for many boomers – the age at which the full Social Security benefit is available); age 70 (the age to which delayed retirement credits or DRCs can be earned if you delay taking your benefit after your Full Retirement Age).

Some election strategies are age dependent. There are elections you can make at age 66 that you cannot make between the ages of 62 and 66. For example, if you elect to begin your Social Security benefit at age 64, the Social Security Administration will assume you are filing for your own worker's benefit, not your spousal benefit. Before age 66 you cannot limit your application to just your spousal benefit. However, at age 66 up to age 70 you can restrict your application to just your spousal benefit.

Why would you want to restrict your application to just your spousal benefit at age 66? Because worker benefits have one big advantage spousal benefits do not have — *Delayed Retirement Credit (DRCs)*. For every year a worker delays receipt of his or her worker's benefit, the monthly payment is increased by 8 percent. In other words, Jeanie can increase her own worker's benefit by 32 percent by delaying receipt to age 70. On the other hand, spousal benefits do not get the benefit of DRCs. Even if the spouse delays receipt of his or her benefits to age 70, the spousal benefit will be fixed at 50% of the benefit paid to the worker at Full Retirement Age.

For example, if Jean's Full Retirement Benefit is $2,000 per month, her husband John's spousal benefit is $1,000 per month (50% of $2,000). If Jean waits until age 70 to collect her Social Security benefit, her payment will increase to $2,640 (4 year delay; 8% increase for each year of delay equals a total DRC of 32%; $2,000 times 32% equals $640; $2,000 plus $640 equals $2,640). John's spousal benefit will still be limited to $1,000 (adjusted, however, for inflation). In other words, his spousal benefit is not $2,640 times 50% or $1,320. John does not benefit from Jean's DRCs; therefore, his best strategy would be to take his spousal benefit at age 66. If he has earned his own worker's benefit he can switch to that at age 70. This allows John's worker benefit to grow by 32% thanks to DRCs.

Some readers may say, "Hey, just a darn minute. How can John file for his spousal benefit if Jean waits to age 70 to file for her benefit?" Excellent point! A spouse cannot file for his or her spousal benefit unless the spouse has filed for his or

---

American Bandstand

Dick Clark's name is synonymous with the teen music and dance show, *American Bandstand*. But Clark (1929 – 2012), did not host the show during its first four years of broadcasting. Before that Bob Horn (1916-1966) hosted the show, known as *Bandstand*, from 1952 to 1956 when Clark took over. It was Horn who actually came up with the format that made American Bandstand an icon – teenagers dancing on camera while popular songs were played. Eventually live performers were added but typically lip-synched their hits. In a famous segment, Clark would interview teens and ask them to give a rating to a song. The program started in Philadelphia as a local show but was picked up nationally in 1957. It ran until 1989.

---

her worker's benefit. Jean can, however, do a "file and suspend" to enable John to file for his spousal benefit. But Jean can make the "file and suspend election" only when she reaches age 66; not before. Knowing these rules can make you money – and is something your advisor should be able to explain to you.

Bottom line: Many strategies are age dependent – be aware of what elections you may or may not make at certain ages. For this reason, you will want to meet with an advisor before age 62 so you don't make the wrong election decision!

Has an Election Been Made?

When planning for their Social Security benefit, a couple will have the maximum flexibility if neither has made an election yet. It is important that you seek guidance before making an election.

For example, most Social Security planners focus on the election made by the higher earning spouse. But let's turn traditional planning on its head. Instead of the higher earning spouse filing for his or her benefit allowing the lower earning spouse to file for a spousal benefit, let's have the lower earning spouse file for his or her benefit first. The higher earning spouse will file for a spousal benefit and allow his Social Security benefit to grow through DRCs. This would not be possible if the higher earning spouse first files for her benefit. Also, keep in mind both spouses cannot file for a spousal benefit based on the other's work history at the same time.

Would this strategy work for you and your spouse? Hard to say, but you want to keep all your options open. A good software program will allow you to run various options – even somewhat nontraditional options, and a good advisor will help you navigate the rules.

Bottom line: When it comes to Social Security planning – the operative phrase is not "better late than never." Plan early, preferably before either spouse has made an election. By planning early you give yourself maximum flexibility and you have time to integrate your Social Security plan into your overall retirement plan. See Chapter 9 on income strategies if you delay your Social Security benefit.

Longevity Protection

Odd as it may sound, you do need protection against living too long. And yes, we keep coming back to this topic of longevity protection. It is especially important for the survivor. So, get over it – this is an important and overlooked topic nowadays when everyone is in a hurry to grab their Social Security benefit. If you are married you need to look ahead to the day your spouse becomes a widow or widower.

That brings up an important point – couples' planning must take into account the life expectancy of the *second to die*.

The fact is that the longer you delay taking Social Security benefits, the greater the survivor benefit will be. While spousal benefits do not increase due to DRCs, if the first to die delayed taking his or her Social Security worker's benefit until age 70, the benefit of that delay will benefit the survivor. Let's look at the numbers both before and after taking inflation into account.

Before taking inflation into account - Andy delays taking his Social Security benefit until age 70. His Full Retirement Age benefit was $2,000. Due to DRCs, his monthly payment at age 70 will grow to $2,640. His spouse, Helen, four years younger than Andy, took her spousal benefit at age 66. Her payment was $1,000 per month. Fifteen years later, Andy dies. As the survivor, Ellen will "step into" Andy's monthly benefit of $2,640 but will lose her spousal benefit of $1,000. Their household Social Security will decrease from $3,640 to $2,640 due to the loss of Helen's benefit.

If both Andy and Helen took benefits as *early as possible*, Helen's spousal benefit would be $700 (or 35% of Andy's PIA of $2,000); Andy's would be $1,500. Their household Social Security income at Andy's death will decrease from $2,200 to $1,500.

Comparing the two options (early vs. late election) Helen will receive $1,140 per month more if the late Social Security election were made ($2,640 survivor benefit vs. $1,500 survivor benefit).

If we take inflation into account - That difference of $1,640 (equals $2,640 survivor benefit minus $1,500) would make a tremendous difference to Helen at age 81 when Andy passes.

If we assume a 3% annual inflation rate, the difference is even larger at Andy's death:

Benefit Election	Andy's Benefit at Age 85	Helen's Benefit at Age 81	Household Social Security Benefit
Early as possible	$2,960	$1,382	$4,342
Late as possible	$5,210	$1,974	$7,184
Difference	**$2,250**	$592	**$2,842**

Just before Andy's death, Andy and Helen's total household income by making a late election was greater by **$2,842**. At Andy's passing, Helen will step into Andy's benefit of $5,210 per month; she will lose her spousal benefit of $1,974. As a result of the late election, Helen's monthly income will be **$2,250** larger than it would be had they made the early election ($5,210 minus $2,960). This difference is HUGE and can cover a substantial portion of Helen's additional care costs should it be needed. If Helen is healthy, it can buy some additional nights out with her lady friends.

Note that because the annual inflation adjustment to Andy's benefit is made to a larger number each year due to the late election it grows faster in relation to Helen's benefit providing more inflation adjusted dollars to her each month. OK, we got a little carried away with the math.

Oops, more math – if Andy and Helen make the late benefit election and live to age 85 and 95 respectively, their total cumulative Social Security benefit will be **$654,000 larger** than it would be if they had made the early benefit election. And most of that "extra" money will be paid in the later years of Andy and Helen's life – when they may need it most for rising health care costs.

Bottom line: When planning your separate Social Security elections remember you must consider both of your life expectancies. Planning for the second to die is as important as the financial planning you do for the last years of your life together. Focus on the monthly payments you will receive as a couple and the monthly payment one of you will receive as the survivor.

Sheldon Leonard?

Few Boomers recognize Sheldon Leonard's name but almost all Boomers will remember many of the TV programs he produced over the years. Leonard (1907-1997) was responsible for such shows as:

☐ Make Room for Daddy

☐ The Dick Van Dyke Show

☐ The Andy Griffith Show

☐ I Spy

☐ Gomer Pyle USMC

Leonard (born Leonard Sheldon Bershad) was also an actor. If you ever watched the classic movie, *It's a Wonderful Life*; he plays Nick, the bartender at Martini's Italian restaurant. His famous line is to Clarence the angel as he tries to make up his mind which drink he will order (Clarence decides on "mulled wine, heavy on the cinnamon and light on the cloves." Nick responds with: "Hey, look, mister, we serve hard drinks in here for men who want to get drunk fast. And we don't need any characters around to give the joint atmosphere. Is that clear, or do I have to slip you my left for a convincer?"

CHAPTER SEVEN

Protecting Your Spousal Rights After Divorce

True story (with names changed to protect the poorly informed): Dee is a 58-year-old librarian with three adult children, a son and two daughters. She met with a financial planner hoping to determine whether or not she could afford to retire at age 62. Her goal was to retire and move to a different area of the country to be closer to her children and grandchildren.

One of the first questions her new financial advisor asked was about Dee's marriage history. Dee mentioned that she had been divorced ten years ago after twenty two years of marriage. She had not remarried. She never talked with her ex-husband. Any news about him she found out through one of her children who still stayed in regular touch with him. Her ex was 65 and, according to her son, was not "planning on retiring anytime soon." That may be due, Dee thought, to the two subsequent marriages he went through after their divorce. "I doubt he can afford to retire at this point. He had children with each of the other women." Dee had a vague idea based on a comment made by a work colleague that she could claim benefits based on her ex's work record but since he was not filing for Social Security she "would have to wait to claim any benefits based on his work record."

He was and still is a high earner and she thought his monthly Social Security benefit would be "pretty high." Like many women, she did have her own work history but because she was relatively low paid and took ten years off from the paid labor force to raise her children, her Social Security benefit was less than half of what she expected her husband's benefit would be.

Dee's story, unfortunately, is not unusual – most Social Security beneficiaries do not realize that they have certain "spousal rights" that are not necessarily lost when they divorce.

While Dee was poorly informed she was smart enough to seek out the advice of a professional who could tell her what rights she did have as an ex-spouse.

Dee's Story

Let's look a little closer at Dee's situation to determine what rights she has still retained as an ex-spouse. The relevant facts in her case for our purposes are:

1. She was married to her ex for well over ten years;

2. Their divorce was more than two years ago;

3. She has not remarried;

4. She is under age 60;

5. Her ex remarried twice but those remarriages both ended in divorce;

6. Dee's ex is eligible for Social Security benefits. At his next birthday in two months, he will be age 66 – his Full Retirement Age (FRA).

As we review Dee's situation remember that Social Security is gender neutral. Any rights that Dee has retained are just as applicable to a male that is in Dee's situation.

In order to retain Social Security spousal rights as an ex-spouse, Dee must meet the following checklist of rights for ex-spouses:

Requirements:

- Dee must have been married ten years or more (Yes)
- ☐ There is no such thing as having a "partial right," in other words, 9 years, 11 months and 29 days of marriage doesn't count. Ten years or nothing!

- Must have been divorced for two years or more (Yes)
- ☐ Limits the attractiveness for those willing to obtain a divorce

just to take advantage of some of the rights an ex-spouse is entitled to.

- He is eligible for Social Security benefits and is age 62 or older (Yes)
☐ Her ex will be 66 in 2 months. He is eligible for benefits.

- Dee must not remarry before age 60 (Yes)
☐ Divorced spouse benefits stop if Dee remarries. Dee believes in the old saying that remarriage after divorce is the triumph of hope over experience.

- She must be age 62 (No)
☐ This only impacts her timing of taking a benefit. At age 62 Dee may decide to file for her reduced spousal benefit just as if she and her ex were still married.

As we know from Dee's story, there are plenty of misconceptions about the rights of an ex-spouse. Let's look at a few:

Requirement or Not a Requirement?

1. Her ex must file for his own benefits before Dee can file for hers (*No longer applicable!*) *This is different from the rules that govern married couples. Dee as the ex-spouse need not wait until her ex files for his Social Security benefit. This rule became effective in 1985 but is still not fully understood by ex-spouses.*

2. When Dee decides to file for her benefits as an ex-spouse, she must let her ex know she is doing so (*Not applicable!*) *Her ex-spouse need not know she is filing for her benefit; Dee is under no obligation to tell him. The Social Security Administration will also not tell him.*

3. Dee's benefit will reduce any benefits the other ex-wives will be entitled to. (*Wrong! Wrong!*) *Dee's rights belong to her alone. What Dee receives will not impact the rights or amounts received by her ex's growing list of ex-wives.*

4. If her ex-husband dies before Dee claims her spousal benefits, she loses her claim and must rely on her own worker benefit (*Wrong! Wrong!*) *Common misconception – the benefits Dee is entitled to do not die with her ex. Like a widow, the divorced spouse is entitled to survivor benefits. Even if the marriage was over long ago, survivor benefits are still available to the divorced spouse.*

5. When she applies for her divorced-spouse benefits, she needs to bring her ex's birth certificate, earnings history, his current contact information including address, email address, phone number, his Social Security number and proof of their marriage and divorce. (*No, TMI!*) *TMI – too much information! All Dee needs to do is prove that she was married to her ex. She does not need to know where he is. The Social Security Administration will ask for enough information to locate his records but that needn't be a lot. Dee does not need to know his earnings information.*

So, when Dee turns age 62, what are her options?

Dee can file early for the ex-spouse benefit to which she has the right based on her ex-husband's earnings record. Because Dee is filing for her benefits *before her FRA* (which is age 66), she will be deemed to be filing for her worker's benefit first. If her divorced-spouse benefit is higher, she will receive a "spousal add-on." If her reduced worker's benefit is $600 (her PIA at her FRA is $800; her reduced benefit would be 75% of that number or $600) and her spousal benefit is $750, she will receive:

Her worker's benefit $600

Spousal benefit add-on $150   (equals $750 minus $600)

Total monthly benefit   **$750**

If Dee waits until *after* her FRA to file she can restrict her application to her divorced-spouse benefit. She may wish to do this even if her own worker's benefit is higher. This will allow her worker's benefit to continue to grow due to Delayed Retirement Credits (DRCs). She can then switch from her divorced-spouse benefits to her worker's benefit at age 70 if that is a higher amount.

Some Planning Tips for Dee

If Dee's financial planner does not ask her about prior marriages during their initial interview, it may be time to find another financial planner.

Keep in mind, that if Dee's worker's benefit is higher than her spousal benefit she will typically receive the higher benefit – her worker's benefit. But proper planning may mean delaying any benefit until FRA and then taking the divorced-spouse benefit until age 70. At age 70 she would switch to her own worker's benefit.

Continuing the example above, if Dee were to wait to file for a benefit at age 66, she could receive her divorced-spouse benefit of $750 per month (ignoring inflation) from age 66 to age 70. At age 70 she can switch to her worker's benefit which would grow from $800 to $1,056 thanks to the DRCs (ignoring inflation). She would receive this higher payment for the rest of her life.

Many of the same basic planning concepts that apply to Dee's planning also apply to others:

☐ Is Dee healthy? What is the longevity history in her family? Does she expect to live longer than the average life expectancy? If that is the case, it will make sense for her to delay taking benefits.

☐ Delaying taking her Social Security for as long as possible is a good idea to increase her initial benefit payment and to create greater payments as she ages and possibly becomes frailer.

☐ Dee, however, may not be in a financial position to put off taking a benefit – in that case working with an advisor to identify her best options is imperative.

☐ While more complicated, the death of the ex-spouse does not eliminate the divorced-spouse's benefits. She (or he) is still eligible for survivor benefits.

The *Sting-Ray* turns 50 and 1969's *Easy Rider*

June 1, 2013 was the 50th birthday for the ultimate Boomer bicycle – *The Sting-Ray*. And was it ever cool with its banana seat and the high handle bars. The handle bars were modeled after the high motorcycle handle bars popular at the time. Of course, who can forget the high chopper handle bars of Billy's (Peter Fonda) and Wyatt's (Dennis Hopper) motorcycles in 1969's *Easy Rider*?

CHAPTER EIGHT

Strategies for Singles

In this chapter we discuss Social Security timing strategies for singles – those never married. If you are single but divorced you should also read Chapter 7 on *Protecting Your Spousal Rights*.

Let's get this out of the way first. If you rely solely on the "breakeven point" to decide on the timing of your Social Security election you are making a mistake. A more sophisticated analysis is required that takes into account one of Social Security's greatest attributes: longevity protection.

The fact is that by delaying the start of your Social Security, you are buying a type of longevity insurance. Longevity insurance protects you from outliving your retirement nest egg. Strange as it may seem, one of your biggest retirement risks is *living too long*. After all, your life expectancy at age 65 is not very meaningful for you. It is a number that applies to a big group – everyone in the United States that is age 65. If the life expectancy for your group is 15 years that means 50% of the group will be dead by age 80. The other half of your group will still be alive. And they need money to live. Your goal is to be in the "still alive" group.

The breakeven analysis that is often done to determine "the best time" to begin benefits compares taking a smaller Social Security benefit early (say at age 62) versus taking a larger benefit later – say at Full Retirement Age (FRA) or at age 70.

So, for example, your Full Retirement Age benefit is $1,000 per month. You can receive $750 at age 62; $1,000 at age 66 or $1,320 at age 70. Your "breakeven point" is at approximately 80 years old. In other words, you have to live to at least age 80 for the "delay" strategy to pay off.

Take benefit at age...	Formula	Cumulative Benefit
62	18 years times 12 times $750 per month	$162,000
66	14 years times 12 times $1,000 per month	$168,000
70	10 years times 12 times $1,320 per month	$158,400

The longevity protection offered by Social Security is ignored in the breakeven analysis. Remember, if your life expectancy is age 80 you have a 50% chance of living longer than that. Dying young is not the problem when it comes to retirement planning – living longer than your life expectancy is the problem (as odd as that sounds).

Another happy fact – 45% of Boomers will die of frailty – meaning we will need at least some care near the end of our life. This care is expensive. By delaying Social Security as long as possible, we push more income into our later years when most of us really need it.

Many Boomers ignore this advice and take their benefit much too early. Their financial plan, apparently, is an early death or going back to work in their 80s. Not a good plan.

Despite the facts, most of us will talk ourselves into taking early benefits arguing that:

1. I'd rather have the money in hand today; if I have to cut back on my spending it will be much later. I can live with that. Besides, at age 80 I'll probably be less active and as a result, spending less.

2. You know the old saying, if you remember the 1960s you probably weren't there? That's me. I was there but don't remember all that much. My life was like a skit from a Cheech and Chong album. I abused my body and mind so much, I don't think it will hold out much longer. Better get my benefits early.

3. The Social Security program is going bankrupt, better to get something now rather than nothing later.

4. I am chronically ill and it is unlikely I will live to age 70 much less age 80.

5. My family longevity history is poor – both my parents died in their 50s or early 60s.

6. I can't afford *not* to take benefits - I have no savings or other sources of income. My job was physically demanding and I don't think at age 62 I can keep at it for much longer.

Cheech and Chong

For you younger Boomers, Cheech and Chong were a two man comedy act that was very popular in the early 70s. Their drug-addled brains were the focus of most of their skits. Believe it or not, they are still on tour. Boomers' kids (and grandkids) may know Cheech Marin from his acting career. He was in such movies as *Spy Kids* (2001) and its sequels and does voice overs for cartoons such as *Dora the Explorer*.

Some of the arguments are valid – financial necessity and likely early death due to a diagnosed chronic illness we will concede. The other arguments we may take issue with – but not here.

Single Individuals and the Social Security Decision

The bottom line: the longer you delay taking your Social Security benefit the greater the benefit will be later in life when you may really need the money.

Ted's Example

Ted is 61, never married. He is considering retiring and taking his Social Security benefit at age 62. He will receive a small monthly pension from his employer. He also has savings in his 401(k) plan at work. He is in good health but wants to retire and travel for a few years. He meets with his advisor and describes his hopes for his upcoming retirement. The advisor uses a software program to compare Ted's cumulative Social Security benefits if he took benefits at age 62 versus age 70. The difference? If Ted delays until age 70, his cumulative benefits if he lives to age 95 will be almost $384,000 larger. In addition, his monthly benefit will be $5,255 at age 95 if he chooses delay; it will be just $2,990 if he starts benefits early. The difference of $2,265 (= $5,255 minus $2,990) per month really hit home for Ted. His Dad lived to be 93 while his Mom made it to almost 100. Both needed care near the end of their lives and Ted knew they struggled with the bills (in fact, he helped them pay some of the bills). He realized that the extra money would come in handy if he needed care. Without a wife or adult children to take care of him should he need care he knew he would have to pay for a care giver. *(Assumes a PIA of $1,600 and COLA adjustments of 2.8%)*

Ted decided to hold off taking Social Security until he was age 70. The advisor also pointed out to Ted that the increase in benefit payments were essentially risk-free (ignoring the political risk of Congress reducing benefits). Ted did decide to file and suspend at age 66. Why? By filing for his Social Security benefit and suspending payments he created a source of cash should he need it. For example, should he become ill at age 68 and need cash for his care, he can ask that his suspension of payments be ended and be reinstated. He will receive his current payments as well as retroactive payments back to age 66. No interest is paid by the Social Security Administration, but the cash may come in handy.

Once he made the decision, he and his advisor figured out an income strategy that would help him meet his living expenses between age 62 and age 70. Surprisingly, the hit to his portfolio wasn't as bad as he thought it would be. He had to draw more income from his nest egg due to the delay in taking Social Security benefits, but the funds were adequate to cover the gap. We'll discuss income strategies when you delay your Social Security start date in a subsequent chapter.

Memphis Soul

What is fondly remembered by Boomers as "Memphis Soul" originated with STAX records located (of course) in Memphis, Tennessee. Founded in 1961 by Jim Stewart and his sister Estelle Axton (**St**ewart plus **Ax**ton = STAX) its stars included Otis Redding ((*Sittin'On) the Dock of the Bay*) Isaac Hayes (*Theme from Shaft*), Sam & Dave (*Soul Man*) and The Staple Singers (*Respect Yourself*). The house band was Booker T & the MGs (*Green Onions*). Several members of Booker T & the MGs, Steve Cropper, Willie Hall, Steve Jordan and Donald "Duck" Dunn appeared as members of the Blues Brothers Band in the 1980 film, *The Blues Brothers*.

CHAPTER NINE

Income Planning

We know what you're thinking.

"OK, it makes sense to delay taking my Social Security benefit for as long as possible. Got it - but I have to eat in the meantime. If I delay taking a benefit until age 70 what do I live on until then?"

This is where careful retirement planning comes in. Keep in mind that Social Security and general retirement income planning are just one piece of a good, overall retirement plan.

As Dr. Seuss reminded us in his 1986 book, *You're Only Old Once! A Book for Obsolete Children,* we are, well, only old once ("In those green-pastured mountains of Fotta-fa-Zee everyone feels fine at one hundred and three"). Because we are only old once, we need to get our retirement planning right from the beginning.

Here is where we make the pitch for you to work with an experienced retirement planner. By experienced we mean someone who looks like they don't still live at home with mom and dad.

Warning sign: During your initial meeting, he or she is constantly checking for texts on the smart phone. You know the look, hands under the table, eyes focused on their lap. An occasional nod to make you think you are being listened to.

Needless to say (but we will say it anyway), the financial planner should have expertise in Social Security! It also helps if he or she has access to a computer program that will go through the calculations necessary to maximize your Social Security.

Warning sign: if the advisor only mentions doing the break-even analysis for you, move on to another advisor.

Of course, the calculation can be done by hand. According to Dr. Laurence Kotlikoff, here is the formula that must be used to maximize a married individual's benefit:

B(a)=PIA(a) x (1-e(n)) x (1+d(n)) x Z(a) max((.5 x PIA*(a) – PIA(a) x (1+d(n))) x E(a,q,m),0) x (1-u(a,q,n,m)) x D(a) (go to http://www.forbes.com/sites/kotlikoff/2013/02/21/three-rules-to-higher-social-security-benefits/)

Warning sign: The advisor might be a little technology challenged if they pull out a slide rule to do the calculation.

Ask the advisor if she has a sample report from the software program used to do the calculation. Can she explain it? Is it clear as to its recommendations and your next steps?

Also feel free to test the advisor's knowledge based on what you've learned in this book. For example:

☐ *Can I file for just my spousal benefits before I reach my FRA?* The answer is "no" – when you file after age 62 but before your FRA, the Social Security Administration "deems" you are filing for both your spousal and your own worker's benefit. Remember, we covered this!

☐ **After I begin receiving my spousal benefits at my FRA, can I later switch to receiving my worker benefits at age 70 to take advantage of DRCs?** Use the acronyms FRA and DRC, someone knowledgeable about Social Security won't flinch; a planner that is clueless as to what you mean will probably try to steer you back to the breakeven analysis. The answer of course, is yes.

☐ **What is an acceptable form of DNA I can submit to the Social Security Administration to prove my identity?** Trick question! You don't have to submit your DNA (at least not yet!) to prove your identity.

☐ Now, back to your original question. If you decide to delay your Social Security benefits, how do you live until your benefits begin? Recall, one of the considerations in delaying Social Security is your finances. Let's face it; some of us don't have the financial ability to put off collecting Social Security.

☐ For many others, it may be possible — indeed preferable — to put off collecting Social Security. Your retirement planner must be able to help you plan your retirement income. He or she will collect your basic financial data and incorporate all your other sources of income into your Social Security strategy. He or she must also take into account tax planning, deciding which sources of income to draw on first to minimize overall taxes. As you will learn in the next chapter, your Social Security may be subject to income tax. Remember, it is what you keep that matters!

☐ Your overall retirement income plan will include "bridge planning" – finding the right income sources to get you from your initial retirement to the day you begin collecting Social Security. You may build your income plan for the bridge period around regular distributions from your retirement nest egg or use an annuity.

Is drawing a paycheck part of your retirement plan? In that case, you have to take into account the **earnings test**. If you begin taking benefits before your Full Retirement Age, you may see your benefits reduced if you continue working and drawing a paycheck. Here is what happens: you lose $1 in Social Security benefits for every $2 earned above $15,120 (for 2013 – this threshold goes up every year for inflation). There is a higher threshold that applies in the year you reach your FRA. As of 2013, the threshold in that year is $40,080. So, before deciding on taking an early benefit, think twice if you are going to continue working.

☐ A simple term certain annuity may do the trick to provide you with sufficient income from age 62 to age 66 or age 70. A term certain annuity makes a monthly payment for a given period of time – for example, four years. If you die during the four year payout period any remaining payments go to anyone you designate (such as your spouse). Immediate life annuities or deferred variable annuities may also be sensible alternatives to get you through the bridge period. You may also want to consider annuities with income guarantees. As you can tell — this type of planning quickly becomes very complicated.

- [ ] *Not your Dad's annuity!* — Once you begin to research annuities you will learn quickly that the marketplace has changed. With millions of baby boomers moving from *accumulating* retirement assets to *spending* retirement assets (some genius invented the word "decumulate" which is a $5 word when a 10 cent word such as "spending" will do!) the insurance companies had to respond with products focused on generating income. Traditional fixed annuities, of course, generate guaranteed income. But traditional annuities don't protect against inflation. More fixed annuities are becoming available that do guarantee an increasing stream of income to help you meet the increasing costs of living due to inflation (remember, Social Security also provides cost of living adjustments) but the guarantees can be expensive.

- [ ] Also, with interest rates low many traditional products are not attractive. Even with higher interest rates many deferred annuity buyers want a little more "upside" than interest-based products offer.

- [ ] Enter a new group of products that meet the challenge of a growing need for income and the possibility of asset growth in excess of what traditional annuities provide.

- [ ] *Fixed index annuities* tie growth within the policy to an outside index such as a stock market index (for example, the S&P 500 or indices of foreign stock markets). You get downside protection if the market index drops (in other words, your account does not absorb the loss) and a greater upside potential if the index goes up. This usually results in a gain greater than what you would get with a traditional annuity that just grows the account based on current interest rates.

☐ *Variable annuities* grow based on the investment portfolio you select within your policy. This typically includes stocks, bonds and some cash. Again, the hope is that over long periods of time, your deferred annuity will grow more than a traditional deferred annuity that credits the account periodically with whatever the current interest rate happens to be. But, depending on your policy terms, you may see the account value fall periodically as the markets fall.

☐ What does this have to do with your need for income? Many of these new products have added *income guarantees* to their policies. A guaranteed income means a steady amount of income will be paid that cannot be outlived. It will never go down below what was guaranteed, but has the potential to grow over time. But how does this differ from your Dad's old traditional fixed annuity payments? After all, it also provided a steady stream of income that he could not outlive. But remember, your Dad received the same dollar amount until he died – it did not increase with inflation. The income stream from the new products is guaranteed never to go below a certain level, even in the case of *poor investment returns*. In the case of good investment returns there is the possibility that the monthly payment will increase – and may increase well ahead of inflation.

☐ Policy provisions differ. Work with a knowledgeable retirement planner who can walk you through the ins and outs of the different policies and find a suitable policy that meets your needs. Don't purchase a policy you don't understand. And finally, remember that insurance company guarantees are only as good as the financial strength of the company itself.

☐ ***Implementation is key*** - In addition to helping you plan your retirement income, you advisor must also be able to help you *implement* your overall retirement income strategy and your bridge income strategy. Just *knowing* what to do is not enough; the plan must be put in place.

Soul Train

Soul Train was the brain child of Don Cornelius (1936-2012). An African American journalist inspired by the Civil Rights movement, he wanted to expose soul music to a wider audience using television. Already working at a local Chicago TV station, WCIU-TV, Soul Train first aired on August 17, 1970. Among the first guests were The Chi-Lites (hits included 1971's *Have You Seen Her* and in 1972, *Oh Girl*). The show moved to national syndication in October 1971 and remained in syndication for 35 years.

Remember, you're only old once! Get the help you need to plan for a comfortable retirement. Your best course of action is to work with an experienced retirement planner.

CHAPTER TEN

Yes, Social Security Benefits May Be Taxed

The taxation of Social Security benefits is like a wedgie – the higher your income, the more uncomfortable it becomes. From **50% (a regular wedgie) to 85% (the atomic wedgie)** of your Social Security income may be subject to Federal income tax. For single taxpayers the tax on Social Security benefits begins at just $25,000 of annual income and for married taxpayers the tax begins at $32,000. Careful tax planning can help many taxpayers reduce the tax they pay on their Social Security benefit.

Very few of us made it through adolescence (well, at least very few boys) without giving or being on the receiving end of a wedgie. For those of you who grew up in a wedgie-less environment, you can find additional information online at Wikipedia.

Think of the taxation of Social Security as the wedgie tax. If your income falls below $25,000 (for a single tax filer) or $32,000 (for married filing joint taxpayers) you are safe – no wedgie tax. But as soon as you cross those income thresholds, your wedgie begins.

Underwear starting to feel a little tight? Well, get ready, the greater your income the more uncomfortable you will become. You will move from up to 50% of your Social Security income being included in your taxable income (the *regular wedgie*) to 85% of your Social Security income being included in your taxable income (the feared *atomic wedgie*).

Let's face it, if any Federal government agency was going to give you a wedgie, it had to be the IRS, right?

Until 1983 Social Security benefits were **not** subject to the Federal income tax. That changed in 1983 when Congress passed the first law subjecting up to 50% of Social Security benefits to income taxes. Only taxpayers with income *above* certain thresholds (single taxpayers with income thresholds over $25,000 and married couples filing joint returns with income thresholds over $32,000) would see a portion of their Social Security subject to income tax.

1983 – Willie and Merle team up

Songs we were listening to in 1983 include *Every Breath You Take* by the Police; *Billie Jean* and *Beat It* by Michael Jackson; *Flashdance...what a Feeling* by Irene Cara; *Down Under* by Men At Work. Michael Jackson's album *Thriller* was released in November 1982, going to #1 in 1983. In country music, Willie Nelson and Merle Haggard reached #1 with *Pancho and Lefty* and Reba McEntire had a hit with *Can't Even Get the Blues.*

In 1993 Congress did it again – for single taxpayers with over $34,000 in annual income and married taxpayers with over $44,000 in annual income, up to 85% of their Social Security benefit could be included in their taxable income.

What makes the wedgie tax particularly annoying is that the income thresholds are not adjusted for cost of living increases. For example, the married filing joint threshold of $32,000 has not changed in 30 years. If it had been increased by the same Cost of Living increases that are made annually to Social Security payments, the threshold would be approximately $75,000. Over the years, more and more Social Security beneficiaries have seen their Social Security payments subject to tax. See the table below on where the income thresholds would be if annual cost of living adjustments had been made.

Filing Status	50% Threshold	50% Threshold Indexed*	85% Threshold	85% Threshold Indexed**
Married, filing jointly	$32,000	$75,000	$44,000	$71,900
Single	$25,000	$58,400	$34,000	$55,000

* Since 1983 using same cost of living amount as used to adjust Social Security benefits.
** Since 1993 using same cost of living amount as used to adjust Social Security benefits
   Approximate values.

Below, we briefly describe how the tax on Social Security benefits works. Don't get hung up in the details. You only need a general idea of how the tax works and possible planning opportunities to avoid (or more likely, reduce) the tax on your Social Security benefits. Here goes:

Filing Status: Single Head of Household Qualifying Widow Amount of Income*	Amount of Social Security income included in taxable income	Amount of Social Security income potentially subject to Federal Income Tax: Calculation	Amount of Social Security included in Taxable Income: What It Means to You
$0 to $25,000	None	N/A	$0
$25,000 to $34,000	Up to 50%	$34,000 minus $25,000 equals $9,000; $9,000 times **50%** equals $4,500.	Up to $4,500 of Social Security income may be included in taxable income
Income is over $34,000	Up to 85%	Depending upon taxpayer's annual income, up to 85% of his or her total Social Security income may be included in taxable income	Up to 85% times annual Social Security income (if your income is high enough, you lose the benefit of the 50% inclusion amount in the $25,000 to $32,000 range and *85% of all* Social Security income is included in taxable income).

We are trying not to get into too much detail, but for purposes of calculating the amount of Social Security benefit that will be included in the taxpayer's taxable income, "income" begins with Adjusted Gross Income (or AGI). You may be familiar with AGI – it is the number that shows up on the last line of page 1 or your Form 1040 of your Form 1040A. You add back certain deductions. You also add any tax exempt income. To this number add one-half of your Social Security benefit. The result is "Provisional Income" which is compared to the threshold amount. If Provisional Income exceeds your threshold, you know what's coming!

Filing Status: Married Filing Jointly Amount of Income	Amount of Social Security income included in taxable income	Amount of Social Security income potentially subject to Federal Income Tax: Calculation	Amount of Social Security included in Taxable Income: Summary
$0 to $32,000	None	N/A	$0
$32,000 to $44,000	Up to 50%	$44,000 minus $32,000 equals $12,000; $12,000 times **50%** equals $6,000.	Up to $6,000 of your Social Security income may be included in taxable income
Income is over $44,000	Up to 85%	Depending upon taxpayer's annual income, up to 85% of his or her total Social Security income may be included in taxable income	Up to 85% times annual Social Security income (if you and your spouse's income is high enough, you lose the benefit of the 50% inclusion amount for income in the $32,000 to $44,000 range and *85% of all* Social Security income is included in taxable income).

OK, so what do these numbers mean and is there anything you can do to reduce the amount of income taxation on your Social Security benefit?

It is difficult to completely avoid tax on your Social Security benefits – if for no other reason than the thresholds have not been adjusted for cost of living increases. At the same time, Social Security benefits have been adjusted for cost of living increases pushing you closer and closer to your income threshold even though only ½ of your benefit is used to calculate whether or not you reached the income threshold. In addition, you may have several sources of income that you cannot defer – pensions and Required Minimum Distributions from retirement plans if you are over age 70½ come to mind.

But it is important that you take the tax on your Social Security benefits into account when you are planning for your retirement income. For example:

1. If you have sources of nontaxable income (such as a Roth IRA or a taxable savings account) it may make sense in some years to draw on those accounts to meet your living expenses. Distributions from a Roth IRA are not included in the calculation to determine your threshold income.

2. If you work after your full retirement age, keep in mind your salary and wages — even part time — may push your income over the threshold and subject your Social Security benefits to taxation.

3. When deciding whether or not to delay Social Security to age 70 (discussed elsewhere in this book) you have to take into account whether your other sources of income to help you meet your monthly living expenses (such as distributions from a 401(k) plan) are taxable.

4. Use of nonqualified deferred or immediate annuities may, because of their favorable tax aspects, have a role to play in your income planning (see Chapter 9).

Chapter Eleven

How Social Security Benefits Are Calculated

Your "Primary Insurance Amount" or PIA is the full monthly Social Security payment you receive if you retire and begin taking benefits at your Full Retirement Age or FRA.

Your PIA calculation is easy enough that a fourth grader could do it. So find yourself a fourth grader and let her do the calculation. Here are the functions she will need to perform:

- Multiply
- Add
- Divide
- Multiply (again)
- Add (again)

The Social Security Administration official acronym for this is MADMA. We just made that up.

In some ways, how your Social Security benefit is calculated is the least important topic of all. You can't go back and change anything. It is what it is. But it is useful to have at least a working knowledge about how the number gnomes at the Social Security Administration calculate your benefits.

---

my Social Security

We are going to recommend you set up your own Social Security account until you do it. Go to www.socialsecurity.gov. Create a *my Social Security* account. Log in. You can easily find your work history. This includes all your wages that were reported to Social Security since you began working. Look it over. If there is an error now is the time to fix it. There is information on how to ask the SSA to fix the error. For example, it may show total Social Security covered wages in one year as $0 when you know for sure you worked that year. Of course for some Boomers the late 1960s are a blur. Especially 1969 – the year of Woodstock.

Here we will do a once-over lightly so you know the mechanics.

1. **Multiply:** The SSA maintains a record of your lifetime Social Security reported earnings based on your Social Security number. If you began working in 1977 your earnings will be recorded from that year onward. Of course, in 1977 you were probably earning the minimum wage of approximately $2.30 per hour. If you worked 750 hours that year your total earnings were $1,725. Admit it; you used part of your earnings to go see the new movie starring John Travolta, *Saturday Night Fever*. Immediately afterwards, you ran out to buy your first pair of disco boots. You assured your parents the boots were a good investment - they would never go out of style. There is a problem with using 1977 dollars in the calculation. The dollars are a little out of date. After all, you probably paid just $2.25 to see *Saturday Night Fever*. The cost of living has changed – an average ticket price now is just about $8.00. To make those dollars comparable to 2013 dollars the amount you earned is multiplied by a factor. So, if you are first eligible for a Social Security benefit in 2014, those 1977 dollars will be multiplied by 4.56. $1,725 times 4.56 equals $7,866. In other words, $7,866 buys you today what $1,725 bought you in 1977. You do that for each year to your earnings up to the year you turn 60. Indexing stops after that although your earnings after age 60 are still included in the calculation.

2. **Add:** From your list of adjusted annual Social Security earnings you add together only the top 35 years. If you don't have a full 35 years of such earnings take the top years (say you had only 21 years of earnings). The other 14 years (35 years minus 21 years) are entered as $0 earnings.

3. **Divide:** The result above is divided by 420 (or 35 years times 12 months per year). The result is your Average Indexed Monthly Earnings or AIME.

4. **Multiply (again):** The Social Security benefit formula is designed to provide a disproportionately higher benefit to lower income workers. This is done using a three tiered benefit formula that accrues Social Security benefits at 90%, 32% and 15%. These rates are applied to your AIME. But higher income taxpayers see their benefit rate *decrease* from 90% to as low as 15% as their average earnings *increase*.

The 90%, 32% and 15% benefit rates are applied at dollar amounts referred to as "bend points." The bend points are adjusted annually for inflation. In 2013, the benefit rates are applied to the following dollar amounts:

Benefit %	Bend Points
90%	AIME up to $791
32%	AIME over $791 through $4,768
15%	AIME over $4,768

The monthly Social Security benefit of a higher income earner with AIME of $5,000 would be $2,020 calculated as:

AIME	Benefit %	Monthly Social Security Benefit
Up to $791	90%	$712
Over $791 up through $4,768	32%	$1,273*
Over $4,768	15%	$35**
Primary Earnings Amount (PIA)		$2,020

*$4,768 minus $791 times 32% equals $1,273**$5,000 minus $4,768 times 15% equals $35

5. Add: Add the numbers in the far right column. $712 plus $1,273 plus $35 equals **$2,020**.

The $2,020 is your PIA. This is the amount you will be paid if you begin taking benefits at your FRA. If you take earnings *before* your FRA, this is the number that is reduced; if you delay taking benefits until *after* your FRA but before age 70 your PIA is the number that is increased due to Delayed Retirement Credits or DRCs.

There you go, easy peasy, lemon squeezy!*

---

*Speaking of Trivia

The origin of the phrase "easy peasy, lemon squeezy" is reportedly a British TV ad from the 1960s selling soap. One company turned trivia into a big business. *Trivial Pursuit* might be considered the last great successful board game. The game was released in 1982. You won the game by having an endless store of useless knowledge otherwise known as trivia. In 1984 alone the game sold 20,000,000 units in North America. 1984 turned out to be its peak year. That might be attributable in part to the rise of the video game industry. For post Boomers, this is ancient history but Boomers can remember staring at the video screen in amazement playing some of the following games. In 1980 *Pac-Man* was introduced; *Donkey Kong* in 1981 (which introduced the Mario character); *Mario Brothers* in 1983 and *Super Mario Brothers* in 1985 all became best sellers. A variety of Trivial Pursuit electronic versions have been introduced over the years but the game has yet to reclaim its glory years of the 1980s. Of course, who can forget The *Bubble Boy* episode of the TV show, *Seinfeld*, broadcast on October 7, 1992? In it, George gets in a fight with the Bubble Boy over the correct answer to a Trivial Pursuit question ("Who invaded Spain in the eighth century?" George insists it was "the Moops" as printed on the Trivial Pursuit card. The bubble boy insists it was "the Moors" and the Trivial Pursuit card had a misprint. "That's not Moops, you jerk, it's Moors. It's a misprint.")

CHAPTER TWELVE

When Your Benefits May Be Reduced

Here is the good news: if you or your spouse has never earned "uncovered wages" you don't have to read this chapter. So you can move along, nothing to see here.

Here is the bad news: if you and/or your spouse have earned "uncovered wages" you may find upon reading this chapter that your Social Security benefits are reduced. And no, skipping this chapter will not help.

Clarification: Uncovered wages do not include cash paid to you "under the table" for work you did and failed to report for Federal income tax purposes. Needless to say, don't look for these types of payments to be included in your Social Security earnings history.

Two rules can substantially reduce Social Security benefits. The first rule is the Government Pension Offset (GPO). The second is the Windfall Elimination Provision (WEP). Because either of these rules can have a drastic *negative* impact on your Social Security benefit we will explain the provisions in some detail.

The GPO and the WEP *impact only payments made to* the individual who earned uncovered wages during his or her working years. The WEP reduces the Social Security worker's benefit paid to that individual with uncovered wages. The GPO reduces (and in some cases, eliminates) any spousal or survivor benefit paid to the individual with uncovered wages.

The chart following is a summary of how payments are affected:

Who is affected	Can Social Security worker's benefit payment be reduced by the WEP?	Can Social Security spousal or survivor payment be reduced or eliminated by the GPO?
Worker who earned *only* uncovered wages during his or her working years	Not applicable	Yes
Worker with a mix of uncovered wages and covered wages received during his or her working years. The covered wages were sufficient to earn the worker his or her own Social Security benefit.	Yes	Not applicable
Worker with uncovered wages receiving spousal benefits.	Not applicable	Yes
Worker with uncovered wages receiving a survivor (widow's or widower's) benefit	Not applicable	Yes

Both the WEP and GPO rules apply to government employees (including school teachers) who earned a pension based on wages not covered by Social Security. Many of these workers are unaware that they are subject to the WEP, the GPO or both. The Social Security statement available through the *my Social Security* account (remember, create an account at www.socialsecurity. gov) contains only a general comment regarding the WEP and the GPO. The recipient is not told if he or she is subject to these rules. The recipient sees only his or her Social Security benefit calculated *before* the reduction. Because the reduction can be substantial many participants greatly overestimate their Social Security benefit.

The GPO

The GPO applies if an individual:

1. Earned wages as a government worker that were not covered by Social Security;

2. Is entitled to receipt of a pension based on their uncovered wages; and

3. Receives either Social Security **spousal or survivor benefits**.

If the GPO applies, the Social Security payment must be reduced by two-thirds of the government pension.

Example: Virginia worked as a school teacher for over 35 years. Her wages were not covered by Social Security. *Virginia meets the first criteria of the GPO applying to her.* She earned a pension that will pay her $1,800 per month at age 65. *She meets the second criteria.* Her husband Niles' wages were covered by Social Security. His Social Security benefit is $2,200. Absent the GPO, Virginia would be entitled to a Social Security spousal benefit of $1,100 per month (50% of $2,200). *She meets the third and final criteria.*

The GPO reduces her spousal benefit by two-thirds of $1,800 or $1,200. Her spousal benefit is equal to $1,100 minus $1,200 or $0 (where the GPO reduction is larger than the spousal benefit, the benefit is reduced to $0).

Impact on survivor benefits – Absent the GPO, should Niles predecease Virginia, she would be entitled to a survivor benefit equal to 100% of Niles' monthly Social Security benefit or $2,200. The GPO, however, requires a reduction in the survivor benefit by two-thirds of her teacher's pension. That leaves a survivor's benefit of $2,200 minus $1,200 (two-thirds of $1,800) or $1,000.

See SSA Publication No. 05-10007 for exceptions available at www.socialsecurity.gov.

The WEP

The best way to understand the WEP is to first understand the Social Security benefit formula. We covered much of this in the previous chapter but repeat it here for purposes of our WEP illustration. For most of you, it will cover ground that you thought you could skip. No such luck if you are impacted by the WEP. Here goes.

The Social Security benefit formula is designed to provide a disproportionately higher benefit to lower income workers. This is done using a three tiered benefit formula that accrues Social Security benefits at 90%, 32% and 15%. These rates are applied to the average earnings of all taxpayers. But higher income taxpayers see their benefit rate *decrease* from 90% to as low as 15% as their average earnings *increase*.

The WEP reduces the 90% benefit rate to as low as 40% for certain Social Security beneficiaries. The 32% and 15% benefit rates are not affected. The WEP reduction can be avoided in whole or in part if the worker had "substantial earnings" covered by Social Security. Substantial earnings are beyond our scope here (don't you wish everything in this chapter was beyond our scope?).

The first step in computing a worker's monthly benefit is computing his or her Average Indexed Monthly Earnings (or AIME) over his or her working life. Only wages covered by Social Security are included in the calculation of the AIME. The AIME is roughly the worker's average monthly earnings covered by Social Security over their working life adjusted for inflation. Once the AIME is computed the actual monthly Social Security benefit is determined.

The 90%, 32% and 15% benefit rates are applied at dollar amounts referred to as "bend points." The bend points are adjusted annually for inflation. In 2013, the benefit rates are applied to the following dollar amounts:

Benefit %	Bend Points
90%	AIME up to $791
32%	AIME over $791 through $4,768
15%	AIME over $4,768

The monthly Social Security benefit of a higher income earner with AIME of $4,000 would be $1,739 calculated as:

AIME	Benefit %	Monthly Social Security Benefit
Up to $791	90%	$712
Over $791 up through $4,768	32%	$1,027*
Total		$1,739

*$4,000 minus $791 times 32% equals $1,027

The WEP reduction is calculated by reducing the 90% benefit rate to as low as 40% for certain participants. While an individual may know he or she is subject to the WEP, they may have little or no idea how much the potential reduction may be.

Let's redo the benefit computed above for the worker with AIME of $4,000 assuming she is subject to the maximum WEP reduction:

AIME	Benefit % Before WEP Reduction	Monthly Benefit Before WEP Reduction	Benefit % After WEP Reduction	Monthly Benefit After WEP Reduction
Up to $791	90%	$712	40%	$316
Over $791 up through $4,768	32%	$1,027	32%	$1,027
Total Monthly Social Security Benefit		$1,739		$1,343

The total monthly reduction due to the WEP in our example is $396 ($1,739 minus $1,343).

Unfortunately, an individual's annual Social Security statement provides only a general statement regarding the WEP. The Social Security monthly benefit shown on the statement is not reduced for the WEP. *This means that the individual will be overestimating his or her monthly Social Security benefit if the proper adjustment is not made.*

For additional information on the WEP and an online calculator you can use to estimate the impact on you go to:

http://www.ssa.gov/retire2/anyPiaWepjs04.htm

For more information on the GPO and the WEP, go to www.socialsecurity.gov. Even better, once there open a *my Social Security* account. Under the Estimated Benefits section there is a brief discussion of both provisions, *but nothing specific as to your situation. You can, however, pull your earnings history from your account and use it in the WEP calculator.*

Conclusion

Well, there you have it – your Roadmap to maximizing your Social Security benefit. Along the way we took a few side trips to recall Baby Boomer music, TV and movie landmarks.

Your takeaways?

- You have flexibility regarding *how* to take your Social Security benefits. You may have earned a benefit as a worker based on your own earnings history and earned benefits as a spouse based on your spouse's (or ex-spouse's) work history. You can even switch from one benefit to another (for example, take your spousal benefit first, later switch to your own worker's benefit).

- If you were divorced, determine if you have any spousal rights from your marriage and if you do, protect them!

- You can elect to take a benefit as early as age 62 or as late as age 70 – or anytime in between. In general, the longer you delay taking a benefit the better off you will be financially.

- Personnel at the Social Security Administration can help you apply for benefits but not *strategize*. For that reason, consider using a knowledgeable advisor who can assist you in identifying all the possible scenarios and selecting the one that makes the most sense for *you* (and if you are married, you and your spouse). The advisor can also assist you with developing an income plan that takes into consideration the delay of Social Security.

Retirement can last thirty years or more. Thirty years is a long time, and you need a plan that will last as long as you do. Frozen for thirty years, Dr. Evil learned that much can change in that amount of time:

Dr. Evil: Gentlemen, I have a plan. It's called blackmail. As you know, the Royal Family of Britain are the wealthiest landowners in the world. Either the Royal Family pays us an exorbitant amount of money or we make it seem that Prince Charles had an affair outside of marriage and would have to divorce.

No. 2: Prince Charles did have an affair. He admitted it and they are now divorced.

Dr. Evil: OK, people, you have to tell me these things. Alright? I've been frozen for thirty years. OK? Throw me a frickin' bone here. I'm the boss. Need the info.

Dr. Evil: Here's the plan. We get the warhead, and we hold the world ransom for...One MILLION DOLLARS!

No.2: Ahem...don't you think we should maybe ask for more than a million dollars? I mean, a million dollars isn't exactly a lot of money these days. Virtucon alone makes over nine billion dollars a year.

Dr. Evil: Really?

No.2: Mm-hmm.

Dr. Evil: That's a number. Okay then. We hold the world ransom for...One hundred BILLION DOLLARS!

Austin Powers International Man of Mystery (1997)

Perhaps the worst retirement planning decision you can make is to focus only on your first few years of retirement and opt to take your Social Security benefits early. Take the time to understand your options and make the right decision for you and your family. Give yourself a better chance of realizing your retirement dreams.